Johannes Brahms

COMPLETE SONGS FOR SOLO VOICE AND PIANO

SERIES I

Johannes Brahms

COMPLETE SONGS FOR SOLO VOICE AND PIANO

SERIES I

From the Breitkopf & Härtel Complete Works Edition
Edited by Eusebius Mandyczewski

with a New Prose Translation of the Texts
by Stanley Appelbaum

Dover Publications, Inc.
New York

Dover's edition of Brahms's solo songs will be complete in four series. Series III and IV are scheduled for publication in mid-1980.

Published in Canada by General Publishing Company, Ltd., 30 Lesmill Road, Don Mills, Toronto, Ontario.
Published in the United Kingdom by Constable and Company, Ltd., 10 Orange Street, London WC2H 7EG.

This Dover edition, first published in 1979, is an unabridged republication of Volume 23 (*Lieder und Gesänge für eine Singstimme mit Klavierbegleitung I*) of *Johannes Brahms; Sämtliche Werke; Ausgabe der Gesellschaft der Musikfreunde in Wien*, originally published by Breitkopf & Härtel, Leipzig, n.d. (Editor's Commentary dated Summer 1926). The front-matter appears here only in English because of space limitations. All translations are by Stanley Appelbaum, prepared specially for the present edition.

International Standard Book Number: 0-486-23820-2
Library of Congress Catalog Card Number: 79-50615

Manufactured in the United States of America
Dover Publications, Inc.
180 Varick Street
New York, N.Y. 10014

CONTENTS

	PAGE
ALPHABETICAL LIST OF SONG TITLES	vi
ALPHABETICAL LIST OF SONG OPENINGS	vii
ALPHABETICAL LIST OF POETS	viii
GLOSSARY OF GERMAN TERMS OCCURRING ON THE MUSIC PAGES	viii
EDITOR'S COMMENTARY	ix
TRANSLATIONS	xiii

SIX SONGS FOR TENOR OR SOPRANO, OP. 3

1. Liebestreu	1
2. Liebe und Frühling I	
Original Version	4
Later Version	6
3. Liebe und Frühling II	8
4. Lied	11
5. In der Fremde	14
6. Lied	16

SIX SONGS FOR SOPRANO OR TENOR, OP. 6

1. Spanisches Lied	20
2. Der Frühling	24
3. Nachwirkung	26
4. Juchhe	28
5. Wie die Wolke nach der Sonne	32
6. Nachtigallen schwingen	34

SIX SONGS, OP. 7

1. Treue Liebe	38
2. Parole	41
3. Anklänge	44
4. Volkslied	46
5. Die Traurende	47
6. Heimkehr	48

SONGS AND BALLADS, OP. 14

1. Vor dem Fenster	50
2. Vom verwundeten Knaben	53
3. Murrays Ermordung	55
4. Ein Sonett	58
5. Trennung	60
6. Gang zur Liebsten	63
7. Ständchen	64
8. Sehnsucht	66

	PAGE
FIVE POEMS, OP. 19	
1. Der Kuss	67
2. Scheiden und Meiden	69
3. In der Ferne	70
4. Der Schmied	73
5. An eine Aeolsharfe	74

SONGS TO TEXTS BY PLATEN AND DAUMER, OP. 32

1. Wie rafft ich mich auf in der Nacht	79
2. Nicht mehr zu dir zu gehen	85
3. Ich schleich umher betrübt und stumm	88
4. Der Strom, der neben mir verrauschte	89
5. Wehe, so willst du mich wieder, hemmende Fessel	92
6. Du sprichst, dass ich mich täuschte	95
7. Bitteres zu sagen denkst du	98
8. So stehn wir, ich und meine Weide	100
9. Wie bist du, meine Königin	103

BALLADS FROM TIECK'S *Magelone*, OP. 33

1. Keinen hat es noch gereut	107
2. Traun! Bogen und Pfeil sind gut für den Feind	116
3. Sind es Schmerzen, sind es Freuden	119
4. Liebe kam aus fernen Landen	126
5. So willst du des Armen dich gnädig erbarmen?	132
6. Wie soll ich die Freude, die Wonne denn tragen?	136
7. War es dir, dem diese Lippen bebten	147
8. Wir müssen uns trennen	152
9. Ruhe, Süssliebchen, im Schatten der grünen, dämmernden Nacht	158
10. Verzweiflung	165
11. Wie schnell verschwindet so Licht als Glanz	171
12. Muss es eine Trennung geben	175
13. Sulima	178
14. Wie froh und frisch mein Sinn sich hebt	183
15. Treue Liebe dauert lange	189

ALPHABETICAL LIST OF SONG TITLES

	PAGE		PAGE
An eine Aeolsharfe	74	Lied	11, 16
Anklänge	44	Murrays Ermordung	55
Der Frühling	24	Nachwirkung	26
Der Kuss	67	Parole	41
Der Schmied	73	Scheiden und Meiden	69
Die Traurende	47	Sehnsucht	66
Ein Sonett	58	Spanisches Lied	20
Gang zur Liebsten	63	Ständchen	64
Heimkehr	48	Sulima	178
In der Ferne	70	Trennung	60
In der Fremde	14	Treue Liebe	38
Juchhe	28	Verzweiflung	165
Liebestreu	1	Volkslied	46
Liebe und Frühling I	4, 6	Vom verwundeten Knaben	53
Liebe und Frühling II	8	Vor dem Fenster	50

ALPHABETICAL LIST OF SONG OPENINGS

	PAGE
Ach könnt ich, könnt ich vergessen sie	58
Angelehnt an die Epheuwand	74
Aus der Heimat hinter den Blitzen rot	14
Bitteres zu sagen denkst du	98
Der Strom, der neben mir verrauschte	89
Des Abends kann ich nicht schlafen gehn	63
Die Schwälble ziehet fort	46
Du sprichst, dass ich mich täuschte	95
Ein Mägdlein sass am Meeresstrand	38
Es lockt und säuselt um den Baum	24
Es wollt ein Mädchen früh aufstehn	53
Geliebter, wo zaudert dein irrender Fuss?	178
Gut Nacht, mein liebster Schatz	64
Ich hör meinen Schatz	73
Ich muss hinaus, ich muss zu dir	8
Ich schleich umher betrübt und stumm	88
In dem Schatten meiner Locken	20
Keinen hat es noch gereut	107
Liebe kam aus fernen Landen	126
Lindes Rauschen in den Wipfeln	16
Mei Mueter mag mi net	47
Mein Schatz ist nicht da	66
Muss es eine Trennung geben	175
Nachtigallen schwingen lustig ihr Gefieder	34
Nicht mehr zu dir zu gehen, beschloss ich	85
O brich nicht, Steg	48
O Hochland und o Südland	55
O versenk, o versenk dein Leid	1

	PAGE
Ruhe, Süssliebchen, im Schatten	158
Sie ist gegangen, die Wonnen versanken	26
Sie stand wohl am Fensterbogen	41
Sind es Schmerzen, sind es Freuden	119
So soll ich dich nun meiden	69
So stehn wir, ich und meine Weide	100
So tönet denn, schäumende Wellen	165
So willst du des Armen dich gnädig erbarmen?	132
Soll sich der Mond nicht heller scheinen	50
Traun! Bogen und Pfeil sind gut für den Feind	116
Treue Liebe dauert lange	189
Unter Blüten des Mais spielt ich	67
Wach auf, du junger Gesell	60
War es dir, dem diese Lippen bebten	147
Wehe, so willst du mich wieder, hemmende Fessel, umfangen	92
Weit über das Feld durch die Lüfte	11
Wie bist du, meine Königin	103
Wie die Wolke nach der Sonne	32
Wie froh und frisch mein Sinn sich hebt	183
Wie ist doch die Erde so schön	28
Wie rafft ich mich auf in der Nacht	79
Wie schnell verschwindet so Licht als Glanz	171
Wie sich Rebenranken schwingen	4, 6
Wie soll ich die Freude, die Wonne denn tragen?	136
Will ruhen unter den Bäumen hier	70
Wir müssen uns trennen, geliebtes Saitenspiel	152

ALPHABETICAL LIST OF POETS

The poets are German unless otherwise stated.

PAGE

Bodenstedt, Friedrich Martin von (1819–1892)   11
Daumer, Georg Friedrich (1800–1875)   85, 98, 100, 103
Eichendorff, Joseph von (1788–1857)   14, 16, 41, 44
Ferrand, Eduard   38
Hafiz (Persian, ca. 1327–1390)   98, 100, 103
Herder, Johann Gottfried von (1744–1803)   55, 58
Heyse, Paul von (1830–1914)   20
Hoffmann von Fallersleben, August Heinrich (1798–1874)   4, 6, 8, 32, 34

PAGE

Hölty, Ludwig (1748–1776)   67
Meissner, Alfred von (1822–1885)   26
Mörike, Eduard (1804–1875)   74
Platen, August von (1796–1835)   79, 88, 89, 92, 95
Reinick, Robert (1805–1852)   1, 28
Rousseau, Jean-Baptiste (French, 1670–1741)   24
Thibau(l)t IV (French, 1201–1253)   58
Tieck, Ludwig (1773–1853)   107–194
Uhland, Ludwig (1787–1862)   48, 69, 70, 73

GLOSSARY OF GERMAN TERMS OCCURRING ON THE MUSIC PAGES

Bewegt = animatedly
Etwas langsam = somewhat slowly
In gehender Bewegung = at a walking pace
Kräftig = powerfully
Langsam = slowly
Langsam, sehr innig = slowly, very fervently
Lebhaft = vivaciously
Mit feurigem Schwung = with fiery impetus
Nicht zu langsam und mit starkem Ausdruck = not too
   slowly, and very expressively

Sehr schnell = very fast
Sehr langsam = very slowly
sehr zart und innig = very tenderly and fervently
Singstimme = voice
Spätere Fassung = later version
träumerisch = dreamily
Ursprüngliche Fassung = original version
Zart, heimlich = tenderly, secretively
Ziemlich langsam = fairly slowly

EDITOR'S COMMENTARY

Editor's Commentary
SIX SONGS, OP. 3

Source Texts: 1. The composer's personal working copy of the first edition, in the possession of the Gesellschaft der Musikfreunde in Vienna. This edition was published in 1854 with the title "Sechs Gesänge für eine Tenor- oder Sopranstimme mit Pianofortebegleitung componirt und Bettina von Arnim gewidmet von Johannes Brahms. op. 3. Leipzig bei Breitkopf und Härtel"; publication number 8835.

2. The second edition. This appeared in the collection "Lieder und Gesänge für eine Singstimme mit Begleitung des Pianoforte von Johannes Brahms," published by N. Simrock, Berlin; publication number 8983.

Remarks: The first edition has only German text; the second, German and English. In the first, the vocal part has an unusually large number of dynamic and tempo markings, which naturally are the same as those in the piano part. In the second edition, Brahms deleted most of these as being obvious. But the conscientiousness, not to say the painful care, with which the vocal part is marked, is so typical of the young Brahms that we follow the first edition in this point. As Opp. 3, 6 and 7 were successively published, this extreme care gradually abated. But for the second edition of Op. 3 Brahms made considerable changes in the second song. Both versions are given here. It is evident at first glance that the original version, in line with the title of the set, was primarily conceived for a tenor; the second version is no doubt due to the acquired knowledge that this type of song is generally sung more often by women.

SIX SONGS, OP. 6

Source Text: The composer's personal copy of the first edition. Same ownership as for Op. 3. This edition was published in 1853 with the title "Sechs Gesänge für eine Sopran- oder Tenor-Stimme mit Begleitung des Pianoforte componirt und den Fräulein Luise und Minna Japha zugeeignet von Johannes Brahms. op. 6. Leipzig, Verlag von Bartolf Senff"; publication numbers 94–100.

Remarks: The composer's copy shows a characteristic correction: in No. 1 ("Spanish Song") Brahms later changed the printed $e^2c\sharp^2$ of the vocal part, in mm. 6 and 8 of the E-flat major section, to $e^2g\sharp^1$, to avoid the octaves with the bass; he did the same at the repetition.

SIX SONGS, OP. 7

Source Texts: 1. The composer's personal copy of the first edition, in the possession of the Gesellschaft der Musikfreunde in Vienna. This edition was published in 1854 with the title "Sechs Gesänge für eine Singstimme mit Begleitung des Pianoforte componirt und Albert Dietrich gewidmet von Johannes Brahms. op. 7. Leipzig, bei Breitkopf und Härtel"; publication number 8946.

2. The second edition. This appeared in the collection cited under Op. 3, with the publication number 8990.

Remarks: The two texts differ in the same way as those of Op. 3. Here too we follow the first edition. All that needs to be added is that in the first edition the tempo of No. 3 is incorrectly given as "Andante molto."

SONGS AND BALLADS, OP. 14

Source Texts: 1. The composer's personal copy of the first edition. Same ownership as for Op. 7. This edition was published in 1861 with the title "Lieder und Romanzen für eine Singstimme mit Begleitung des Pianoforte von Johannes Brahms. op. 14. Winterthur, J. Rieter-Biedermann"; publication number 169.

2. The MS copy for the engraver of the first edition, in the possession of Geheimrat Prof. W. His in Berlin-Grunewald. An oblong booklet of 16 leaves of nine-staff music paper. No. 3 is autograph, the other songs are a carefully checked copy. Title: "8 Lieder und Romanzen [the rest as above] von Johannes Brahms. op." The "8" was deleted by the publisher, the opus number entered later by the composer. The songs begin on the third page. The booklet is comprised of individual sheets, with each song on one sheet. A few pages are blank, a few bear only the title.

Remarks: The two source texts agree perfectly. Brahms later noted in his printed copy that at the end of the second and beginning of the third stanza of No. 2, the original wording is not "Knab'n" and "Knab," but "Mann." We retain the former version, which corresponds to the title. In No. 8, we adopt a few small changes added later by the composer in his printed copy: the first edition gives the second note (8th-note) in the vocal part, mm. 12 and 14, as a^1, exactly the same as the accompaniment; similarly, it gives the second note (8th-note) in m. 22 as b^1; it gives m. 20 as:

FIVE POEMS, OP. 19

Source Texts: 1. The original MS, in the possession of the firm of N. Simrock in Berlin. An oblong booklet of four sheets of nine-staff music paper; a clean copy. On the first page, the title: "Der Kuss. v. Ludwig Hölty. Scheiden und Meiden. In der Ferne. Der Schmied. v. Ludw. Uhland. An eine Aeols-Harfe v. Ed. Mörike. 5

Gedichte in Musik gesetzt für eine Singstimme mit Begleitung des Pianoforte von Johannes Brahms, op. 19." The MS lacks the fifth song; it has retained outward traces of it.

2. The composer's personal copy of the first edition, in the possession of the Gesellschaft der Musikfreunde in Vienna. This edition was published in 1862 with the title "Fünf Gedichte für eine Singstimme mit Begleitung des Pianoforte componirt von Johannes Brahms. op. 19. Verlag von N. Simrock in Berlin"; publication number 6205.

Remarks: According to Max Friedländer ("Brahms' Lieder. Einführung in seine Gesänge," N. Simrock, Berlin and Leipzig, 1922), the composer's copy of the book is a later printing of the first edition, since the vocal part contains relatively few dynamic and tempo markings. The vocal indications mentioned by Friedländer as deleted by Brahms are restored here on the basis of the MS to show the original form of the notation (see Remarks to Op. 3); it is easy to think them away, and they can be followed almost instinctively as the obvious thing to do.

In No. 3, page 4, m. 4 from below, the MS gives the piano right hand

and correspondingly, page 6, m. 5:

For the first edition the composer softened this.

SONGS, OP. 32

Source Texts: 1. The composer's original MS, in the possession of Jérôme Stonborough in Vienna. Unfortunately incomplete. An oblong booklet of four leaves of ten-staff music paper. On the first page, only the title; the second page blank; on the following pages, songs 7–9; 1–6 are missing. The autograph title reads: "Lieder und Gesänge von Platen und Daumer in Musik gesetzt für eine Singstimme mit Begleitung des Pianoforte von Johannes Brahms. op. 32 (Nr. 1–4, 5–9)." Originally Brahms had written "componirt." Next to this are the publisher's instructions to the engraver. The division into plates shows as well that this MS was the engraving copy.

2. The composer's personal copy of the first edition, in the possession of the Gesellschaft der Musikfreunde in Vienna. This edition appeared in 1864 with the title "Lieder u. Gesänge von Aug. v. Platen und G. F. Daumer in Musik gesetzt für eine Singstimme mit Begleitung des Pianoforte von Johannes Brahms. op. 32. Heft 1. Heft 2. Leipzig und Winterthur, J. Rieter-Biedermann"; publication number 400ab.

Remark: For Nos. 7–9 the two source texts agree perfectly, and since the composer's copy of the first edition corrects only one printing error, it was possible to consider the first edition as completely reliable.

BALLADS FROM TIECK'S "MAGELONE," OP. 33

Source Texts: 1. The original MSS of Nos. 2, 7, 9, 14 and 15, in the possession of Jérôme Stonborough in Vienna; that of No. 5, in the possession of Mrs. von

Balassa in Budapest; and that of No. 12, in the possession of the Gesellschaft der Musikfreunde in Vienna—all on oblong nine-staff music paper, each number appearing individually, 14 and 15 with the notation at the end: "Mai 69."

2. The composer's personal copy of the first edition; this was published between 1865 and 1869, in five parts of three songs each, with the title "Julius Stockhausen gewidmet. Romanzen aus L. Tieck's Magelone für eine Singstimme mit Pianoforte componirt von Johannes Brahms. op. 33. Eigenthum des Verlegers. Leipzig und Winterthur, J. Rieter-Biedermann. 5 Hefte zu 1 Thlr"; publication numbers 401a–e.

Remarks: We have followed the first edition and the alterations later entered by Brahms in his personal copy. Individual items to be noted:

No. 2 originally had a somewhat longer ending:

In No. 3, at the return of the common time, Brahms changed the first four measures of the vocal part (not of the piano part). The first edition has:

Something similar happened in No. 4; in the Poco vivace section, the first edition has:

At first Brahms changed this to:

and tried to make a corresponding alteration in the parallel passage 21 measures later. But he gave this up at once, evidently because of the text, and changed the first passage again. We follow this final wish.

In No. 5, the MS gives two versions for the end of the third stanza:

In the first edition, the composer decided in favor of the small notes.

The MS of No. 7, in contrast to those mentioned so far, is a clean copy and gives the song in *D-flat* major. This is explained by the remark at the end: "Fräulein Ottilie Hauer zu freundlichem Gedenken Joh⁵ Brahms." Here the tempo is Poco Allegro, and the performance indications in the first measure are "poco *f*" and "con passione"; the accompaniment figure in the left hand contains a syncopation:

which is retained in this form throughout the piece. M. 13 shows a slight divergence from the printed version; the right hand in the piano part has:

Similarly, 13 measures later, the right hand has:

which recurs in exactly this way in the later repetitions. With the second stanza, the voice enters a measure later:

According to the MS, the beginning of the final section of the song first read:

This was changed to:

and it appears that way in the first edition. But in his personal copy Brahms made another change. In the MS, the last four measures of the vocal part have the text "ein Leben in schönsten Tod"; in the first edition, "im schönsten, schönsten Tod." Also, the MS does not contain the last measure of the postlude; it ends with the preceding chord, which lacks the ties and bears the fermata.

In No. 8, the personal copy does away with an error in the accompaniment that disturbs the sense.

In the MS, No. 9 bears the subtitle "Schlummerlied." A change in the last measures of the vocal part

was attempted but apparently soon rejected.

No. 12 originally had no prelude; it was added to the MS at some later moment. The group of three quarter-notes (created by the syncopation) in the first interlude and, correspondingly, in the next-to-last measure of the last stanza of the vocal part, is marked as a triplet in both source texts, although it is not one. The indication must mean that this group is to executed more like a triplet, without stressing the syncopated nature of the

second member. In the one-measure interlude after the third stanza, the MS gives the left hand of the piano part

In No. 13, the antepenultimate measure of the eighth (last) stanza diverges slightly from the antepenultimate measure of the fourth stanza (which is otherwise constructed exactly analogously) at the forte in the accompaniment that arises from the preceding crescendo: here, the pure *f♯* triad; there, the diminished triad. Perhaps, in spite of all the care that was taken, this is a printing error that was overlooked; but perhaps the intention was to follow the text more closely at this high point of the melody, giving the "entfliehn" the dissonance and the "Liebe" the consonance. Unfortunately the MS of this song is not available.

In the MS, the end of No. 14 bears the date "Mai 69."

In No. 15, the original bass of the accompaniment in m. 10 was

In the second stanza, Brahms originally wrote "fodern," like Tieck, and changed it for the first edition. In the animated alla-breve section, before the "a tempo," where the vocal part has the "ad. libit.," both source texts specifically mark the piano part with the obvious "colla voce" (*c. v.*). Seventeen measures after this "a tempo," the vocal part enters a measure earlier in the MS:

The passage that follows, up to the "Tempo I," originally had the following form:

As in No. 14, the MS has "Mai 1869" at the end.

Eusebius Mandyczewski

Vienna, Summer 1926

TRANSLATIONS

SIX SONGS FOR TENOR OR SOPRANO
VOICE AND PIANO, OP. 3
Dedicated to Bettina von Arnim; published 1854

1. LIEBESTREU (Fidelity in Love; text by Reinick)

"Oh, sink, oh, sink your sorrow, my child, in the sea, in the deep sea!" "A stone may rest on the ocean bottom; my sorrow always rises to the surface." "And the love that you bear in your heart, break it off, break it off, my child!" "Even if the flower dies when it is broken off, faithful love does not die so quickly." "And your faith, and your faith, it was just a word, out into the wind with it!" "Oh, Mother, even if the cliff face splinters in the wind, my faith endures it, endures, endures it."

2. LIEBE UND FRÜHLING I (Love and Spring, I; text by Hoffmann von Fallersleben; two consecutive versions)

As vine tendrils tremble in the breath of the mild breezes, as white bindweeds curl airily about the rosebush—that is how my thoughts by day and night, joyful with springtime, calmly and gently embrace and twine around a beloved and dear image, my thoughts by day and night around a beloved and dear image.

3. LIEBE UND FRÜHLING II (Love and Spring, II; text by Hoffmann von Fallersleben)

I must leave my house, I must go to you, I must tell you this myself: you are my springtime, only you, in these bright days. I don't want to see the roses any more, nor the green meadows; I no longer want to go to the forest for fragrance and nature's sounds and the shade. I no longer want the coolness of the breezes, nor the murmur of the waves; I no longer want to see the birds fly nor hear them sing. I want to leave my house, I want to go to you, I want to tell you this myself: you are my springtime, only you, in these bright days.

4. LIED (Song; from the poem *Ivan* by Bodenstedt)

Far over the fields, high through the sky, a mighty vulture flew after prey. By the river bank in the fresh grass sat a young white-winged dove; oh, hide, little dove, in the green forest, or else the greedy vulture will soon gobble you up! A seagull flies high above the Volga and, spying prey, circles with a rocking motion. Oh, keep hidden in the water, little fish, so the spying gull doesn't discover you! If you ascend, it will descend and make you its prey and bring you to the grave. Ah, you moist green earth! Open wide and set my stormy heart at rest! Blue cloth of heaven, adorned with the little stars, oh, dry the tears from my eyes! Heaven, assist the poor, patiently waiting girl! My heart is breaking, my heart is breaking from pain and sorrow, from pain and sorrow!

5. IN DER FREMDE (Far from Home; text by Eichendorff)

Behind the red lightning-flashes, the clouds are coming from the direction of my home. But Father and Mother are long dead, no one there knows me any more, no one there knows me any more. How soon, ah, how soon that peaceful time will come when I, too, shall rest and the beautiful lonely forest will rustle over my head, and no one here will know me any more, no one here will know me any more.

6. LIED (Song; text by Eichendorff)

You soft rustling in the treetops, you little birds who are flying far away, you streams that come from the silent peaks, tell me where my home is, tell me where my home is. Today in a dream I saw it again, and from every mountain such a warm greeting came down to meet me that I began to weep, that I began to weep. Ah, here on the unfamiliar mountaintops, people, streams, cliffs and trees are all like a dream to me, like a dream! You cheerful birds in the treetops, you young men there in the valley, bring a thousand, thousand greetings from me in these strange mountaintops to my home!

SIX SONGS FOR SOPRANO OR TENOR
VOICE AND PIANO, OP. 6
Dedicated to Misses Luise and Minna Japha;
published 1853

1. SPANISCHES LIED (Spanish Song; German text by Heyse)

In the shadow of my tresses my lover has fallen asleep; shall I awaken him now? Oh, no! Oh, no! Oh, no! Every day early in the morning I have carefully combed my curly hair, but my efforts go for nothing because the wind dishevels it; shadow of tresses and humming of wind have lulled my lover to sleep; shall I awaken him now? Oh, no! Oh, no! Oh, no! I must put up with his telling me how grieved he is at yearning for so long now, how this brown cheek of mine gives him life and takes it away. And he calls me his serpent, and yet he fell asleep beside me; shall I awaken him now? Oh, no! Oh, no! Oh, no!

2. DER FRÜHLING (Springtime; text by J.-B. Rousseau)

The breezes murmur temptingly around the tree: awaken from your sleep and your dream; the winter has thawed, the winter has thawed. Now it looks up vigorously, its eyes gaze brightly upon the sun's golden light, upon the sun's golden light.

A gentle, tepid stirring, rocked in the mass of clouds, descends like a heavenly fragrance, like a heavenly fragrance. Now all the flowers awaken, now the melting sigh of the birds resounds, now springtime is returning, now springtime is returning.

The wind wafts the pollen from calyx to calyx, from leaf to leaf, all through the days and nights, all through the days and nights. You, too, my heart, take wing and fly away, seek out a heart in this place and that; perhaps you'll find the right one, perhaps you'll find the right one.

3. NACHWIRKUNG (Aftereffect; text by Meissner)

She has gone away, all bliss has vanished; now my cheeks are hot, now my tears pour down; my sick, feverish mind is reeling, my heart pounds with wishing and longing, my heart pounds with wishing and longing.

If formerly I began my day with thankful prayer and lived through each day in calm delight, now I neglect my work and only dream of the words and glances she used to bestow on me, of the words and glances she used to bestow on me.

Thus do the bees, long after the day has departed, in the whistling night air, through the whistling wind, still cling, as if intoxicated and sunk in rapture, to trembling blossoms of the fragrant lime tree, to trembling blossoms of the fragrant lime tree.

4. JUCHHE (Hurrah!; text by Reinick)

How beautiful the earth actually is, how beautiful! The little birds know it, the little birds know it; they lift their light plumage, they lift their light plumage, and sing such happy songs, and sing, and sing, to the blue heavens, to the heavens, to the blue heavens.

How beautiful the earth actually is, how beautiful! The rivers and lakes know it, the rivers and lakes know it; in their clear mirror they paint the gardens and towns and hills, in their clear mirror they paint the gardens and hills, and the clouds that pass overhead, that pass overhead, and the clouds that pass overhead!

And poets and painters know it, and many other people know it, and many other people know it! And whoever doesn't paint it, sings it; and whoever doesn't sing it, hears music in his heart from pure joy, in his heart from pure joy, from pure joy, hears music in his heart from pure, pure joy!

5. WIE DIE WOLKE NACH DER SONNE (As the Cloud for the Sun; text by Hoffmann von Fallersleben)

As the cloud wanders and yearns for the sun, full of longing, and, warmed through with heavenly rapture, clings dying to its breast:

As the sunflower turns its face to the sun and does not relinquish it until its own eye is clouded in death:

As the eagle, on its path of cloud, yearningly ascends to the vault of heaven and, dazzled by its immersion in sunlight, falls back to earth blinded:

Thus must I, too, long, yearn, gaze and think about seeing you, thus do I want to stare into your eyes and perish from their brightness, and perish, perish from their brightness.

6. NACHTIGALLEN SCHWINGEN (Nightingales Beat; text by Hoffmann von Fallersleben)

Nightingales beat their feathery wings merrily, nightingales sing their old songs. And all the flowers awaken once more to the tuneful sound of all these songs. And my longing becomes a nightingale and flies off into the blossoming world, and asks everywhere of the flowers,

where my, my little flower can be, where my little flower can be. And the nightingales perform their round dance in leafy bowers amid blossoming branches, but I must be silent about all the flowers. I stand among them silently with my sad thoughts: I see one flower that refuses to bloom.

SIX SONGS FOR SOLO VOICE AND PIANO, OP. 7
Dedicated to Albert Dietrich; published 1854

1. TREUE LIEBE (True Love; text by Ferrand)

A girl sat by the seashore and looked into the distance longingly: "Where are you, my beloved, where do you tarry so long? The pressure of my heart gives me no rest. Ah, if you would only come today, my beloved, ah, if you would only come today, my beloved!"

Evening approached, the sun sank at the edge of the sky. "So then, the waves will never bring you back to me? It is in vain that my eyes peer into the distance. Where will I find you again, my beloved, where will I find you again, my beloved?"

The water flatteringly played about her feet like dreams of happy hours; she was drawn into the deep by some silent force. The lovely figure never stood upon the shore again; she found her loved one!

2. PAROLE (Watchword; text by Eichendorff)

She stood at her arched window and sadly braided her hair; the huntsman had gone away, the huntsman was her sweetheart. And when the springtime came and the world was snowy with blossom, she took courage and went out to the green moorland. She puts her ear to the turf, she hears the sound of far-off hoofbeats; that is the deer grazing on the shady mountain slope, on the shady mountain slope. And in the evening the forests rustle, only a shot is still heard from afar off; then she stands still to listen: "That was my sweetheart's greeting! That was my sweetheart's greeting!" Then the streams broke forth from the rocky cliffs, then the birds flew swiftly into the valley! "You companions, wherever you chance to meet him, oh, bring him a thousand greetings from me, a thousand, thousand greetings!"

3. ANKLÄNGE (Reminiscences; text by Eichendorff)

High above the silent heights a house stood in the forest; it was such a lonely sight out there over the woods. In it there sat a girl in the silent evening hour, spinning silken threads for her wedding dress, spinning silken threads for her wedding dress.

4. VOLKSLIED (Folksong)

The little swallow flies away, flies away, far off to some other, other place; and I sit here in sadness; it's an evil, hard time. I wish I could go out into the world, out into the world, because I don't like it here at all, not at all! Oh, come, little swallow, I beg you, I beg you! Show me the way and take me along!

5. DIE TRAURENDE (The Unhappy Girl; folksong)

My mother doesn't love me, and I have no sweetheart; oh, why don't I die? What am I doing here? Yesterday there was a parish fair, but I'm sure nobody looked at me, because I'm so unhappy that I don't dance. Leave alone the three roses that bloom by the little cross: did you know the girl who lies beneath it?

6. HEIMKEHR (Homecoming; text by Uhland)

O footbridge, don't break—you are trembling so! O

cliff, don't crumble—you are threatening so! World, do not perish; sky, don't fall down, sky, don't fall down, until I'm with the girl I love, until I'm with the girl I love, until I'm, until I'm with the girl I love!

SONGS AND BALLADS FOR SOLO VOICE AND PIANO, OP. 14
Published 1861

1. VOR DEM FENSTER (Outside the Window; folksong)
"If the moon doesn't shine too brightly, if the sun doesn't rise too early, I will go out serenading tonight as I've done in the past."

When he stepped out into the street, he began a song and sang, he sang with a beautiful, clear voice, so that his sweetheart jumped out of bed.

"Be quiet, be quiet, my sweetheart, be quiet, be quiet and don't move, or you'll wake up Father, or you'll wake up Mother, and that would be bad for both of us."

"What do I care about your father, what do I care about your mother? I must stand outside your bedroom window, I want to look at my beautiful sweetheart, for whose sake I have to go so far away."

Then the two stood side by side joining their tender lips; the watchman blew his horn. "Farewell, farewell, we must part."

"Oh, parting, one parting after another, parting hurts my young heart; I'll never forget that I have to be separated from my beautiful darling."

2. VOM VERWUNDETEN KNABEN (About the Wounded Boy; folksong)
A girl decided to get up early and take a walk in the green forest. And as she now entered the green forest, she found a wounded boy. The boy was all red with blood, and when she turned aside he was already dead. "Where can I now find two women mourners who will sing funeral chants for my beloved? Where can I now find six youthful knights who will bear my beloved to his grave? How long, then, shall I continue mourning? Until all waters flow together? Yes, all waters will never flow together, so my mourning will have no end."

3. MURRAYS ERMORDUNG (The Assassination of Murray ["Ye highlands and ye lowlands"]; Scottish; from Herder's *Voices of the Nations*)
O highlands, and O southern land! What has happened upon you? Slain is the noble Murray, I shall never see him again, I shall never see him again.

Oh, woe to you, woe to you, Huntley! So faithless, false and bold; you must bring him back to us; you have killed him, you have killed him.

He was a handsome knight in races and tourneys; our Murray was at all times the crowning champion.

He was a handsome knight in war games and ball games; noble Murray was the choicest flower everywhere.

He was a handsome knight in dancing and playing the lute; how unfortunate that noble Murray was pleasing to the Queen!

O, Queen, you will long gaze over the castle wall before you see the handsome Murray riding in the valley, riding in the valley.

4. EIN SONETT (A Sonnet from the Thirteenth Century; German text by Herder, after Thibault)
Oh, if I could only, only forget her, her beautiful, lovely, loving nature, her glance, her friendly mouth! Perhaps I could then grow well! But ah, my heart, my heart can never do so! And yet it is madness to hope for her! And to hover about her gives courage and life, never to draw away. And then, how can I forget her, her beautiful, lovely, loving nature, her glance, her friendly mouth? Much better never to grow well!

5. TRENNUNG (Separation; folksong)
"Awake, awake, you young lad, you have slept so long; outside, the birds are brightly singing, the carter clatters on the road!

"Awake, awake, in a clear voice the watchman has begun to call; when two sweethearts are together, it behooves them to be prudent."

The boy was really drowsy, he slept so long, so sweetly; but the girl was wise and aroused him with her kisses!

Parting, parting is needful; it's as cruel as death, which parts many a pair of red lips and many tender lovers.

The boy leapt onto his steed and departed at a swift trot; for a long time the girl gazed after him; deep sorrow enveloped her!

6. GANG ZUR LIEBSTEN (Visiting His Sweetheart; folksong)
"In the evening I can't go to sleep; I must go to my loved one, I must go to my loved one, even if I stop short outside her door—quite secretly!"

"Who's there? Who's knocking that can awaken me so softly?" "It's your lover; wake up, darling, and let me in—quite secretly!"

"If all the stars were scribes and all the clouds were paper, and they wrote to my darling, they couldn't get all my love into the letter—quite secretly!"

"Oh, if I had feathers like a rooster and could swim like a swan, I'd swim across the Rhine to see my sweetheart—quite secretly!"

7. STÄNDCHEN (Serenade; folksong)
Good night, good night, my darling, good night, sleep well, my dear! Good night, good night, my darling, good night, sleep well, my dear! May all the angels that are in Heaven protect you! Good night, good night, my darling, sleep, sleep peacefully through the night, sleep peacefully through the night!

Sleep well, sleep well and dream of me, dream of me tonight! Sleep well, sleep well and dream of me, dream of me tonight! So that, when I'm asleep, too, my heart will still keep a vigil for you; so that, in a full blaze of love, it may think about you, about you during that time, think about you during that time.

The nightingale is singing in the bushes in the bright moonlight, the nightingale is singing in the bushes in the bright moonlight; the moon shines into your window, peeps into your bedroom; the moon sees you sleeping there, but I, but I must depart alone, but I must depart alone!

8. SEHNSUCHT (Longing; folksong)
My lover isn't here, he's far over the sea, and every time I think of him my heart hurts so badly! The sea is beautifully blue and my heart hurts, and my heart won't get well until my lover returns! The sea is beautifully blue and my heart hurts, and my heart won't get well until my lover returns.

FIVE POEMS FOR SOLO VOICE AND PIANO, OP. 19
Published 1862

1. DER KUSS (The Kiss; text by Hölty)

Beneath blossoms of May I toyed with her hand, caressed her lovingly, caressed her lovingly, gazed at my floating image in the girl's eyes, tremblingly stole the first kiss from her. That kiss now races palpitatingly through my inmost being like a searing fire. Now that you have shot flames of immortality through my lips, give me cooling comfort, give me cooling comfort!

2. SCHEIDEN UND MEIDEN (Parting and Separation; text by Uhland)

So I am now to stay away from you, joy of my life! You kiss me as we part, I press you to my breast!

Oh, darling, is it separation when two people hug and kiss? Oh, darling, is it parting when two people are in close embrace?

3. IN DER FERNE (Far Away; text by Uhland)

I want to rest under the trees here, I so enjoy hearing the little birds. How is it that your song goes so directly to my heart, why does your song go to my heart? What do you know about our love in this far-off place, in this far-off place? I want to rest here on the edge of the brook, where fragrant flowers are sprouting. Who sent you flowers here? Who sent you here? Are you a heartfelt love token from my darling far away, from my darling far away?

4. DER SCHMIED (The Blacksmith; text by Uhland)

I hear my lover, he swings the hammer; the noise and sound penetrate the distance like the ringing of bells through streets and squares. By the blackened hearth my darling sits, but when I pass by, the bellows wheeze, the flames shoot up and flicker around him.

5. AN EINE AEOLSHARFE (To an Aeolian Harp; text by Mörike)

Propped up against the ivy-clad wall of this old terrace, you, the mysterious lute of some air-born muse—begin, once more begin your melodious lament. You come here, winds, from far off, ah, from the fresh green hill-home of the boy I loved so well. And brushing spring blossoms on your way, saturated with fragrances, how sweetly, how sweetly you oppress my heart! And you rustle this way, through the strings, attracted by euphonious melancholy, growing in the course of my longing and dying away again. But all at once, as the wind blows this way more violently, a lovely cry of the harp repeats, to my pleasant alarm, my soul's sudden stirring, and here the full-blown rose, shaken, strews all its petals at my feet.

SONGS TO TEXTS BY PLATEN AND DAUMER FOR SOLO VOICE AND PIANO, OP. 32
Published 1864

1. (Text by Platen)

How I roused myself in the night, in the night, and felt myself drawn onward, onward, felt myself drawn onward. I left the lanes guarded by the watchman, and softly in the night, in the night, walked through the gate with the Gothic arch. The millstream murmured through the rocky gorge; I leaned over the bridge; far below me I observed the waves that were rolling so softly in the night, in the night, but not one of them rolled back, but not one of them rolled back. Above, kindled in infinite number, the stars were turning melodiously in their courses, and with them the moon in pacified splendor; they twinkled softly in the night, in the night, through deceptively remote distances, through deceptively remote distances. I looked up in the night, in the night, and looked down, down again, and looked down again: alas, how you have spent your days, alas, how you have spent your days; now softly in the night, in the night, silence the regret in your pounding heart!

2. (Text by Daumer from *The Moldau*)

I decided not to go to you any more, and I swore it, and I go every evening, because I have lost all my strength, all my strength and all my steadfastness. I would like to stop living, I would like to perish instantly, instantly, and yet I would like to live for you, with you, and never, never die. Oh, speak, say just a word, a single word, a clear word; give me life or death, but please reveal your feelings to me, your true feelings!

3. (Text by Platen)

I drag myself along, worried and mute; you ask—oh, don't ask me why! My heart is shaken by so many sorrows! Is it possible for me to be too gloomy, too gloomy? The tree withers, the fragrance evaporates, the leaves lie so yellow in the flowerbed; a shower pours in violently. Is it possible for me to be too gloomy, too gloomy?

4. (Text By Platen)

The stream that rushed past me, where is it now? The bird to whose song I listened, where is it now? Where is the rose my loved one wore on her heart, and that kiss which intoxicated me, where is it, where is it, where is it now? And that man I used to be, for whom I have long since substituted a different self, where is he, where is he, where is he now? Where is he now?

5. (Text by Platen)

Alas, you want to hold me fast again, you impeding fetters? Up and out into the air, up and out, and out into the air! Let my soul's desiring flow forth, let it flow forth in thundering songs, inhaling, inhaling ethereal fragrance, inhaling ethereal fragrance! Struggle against the wind so it cools your face, greet the sky with joy, greet the sky, the sky with joy! Will feelings of fright stir in the immeasurable expanse? Exhale, exhale the enemy from your breast, exhale, exhale the enemy from your breast!

6. (Text by Platen)

You say I was in error; you swore it solemnly; I know that you were in love, but you are no longer in love, no longer, no longer in love! Your beautiful eyes burned, your kisses burned intensely; you loved me, confess it, but you are no longer in love, no longer, no longer in love! I do not count on a new, faithful return: just admit that you were in love, and after that, love me no longer, and love me, love me no longer!

7. (Translated by Daumer from Hafiz)

You think you are saying bitter things, but you can never give pain, as angry as you are. Your attempts at harsh speeches are wrecked on a coral reef, wrecked on a coral reef; they all become pure acts of grace, because in order to do harm, they must sail past lips that are sweetness itself, that are sweetness itself.

8. (Translated by Daumer from Hafiz)

Unfortunately, these are the terms my darling and I are on. I can never do anything she likes, she can never do anything to give me pain. It irritates her when I adorn her brow with a diadem; I am thankful even for her wrathful answers, as if they were gracious smiles. Unfortunately, these are the terms my darling and I are on, the terms we are on.

9. (Translated by Daumer from Hafiz)

My queen, how rapturous you are when you are gentle and kind! Just smile, and spring fragrances waft through my spirit rapturously, rapturously! The brightness of newly opened roses—shall I compare it to your brightness? Ah, your bloom is beyond all else that blooms, rapturous, rapturous! Walk through lifeless deserts, and green shadows will spread—even if fearful sultriness reigns there without end—rapturously, rapturously. Let me perish in your arms! There death itself, even if the sharpest mortal pains rage through my breast, is rapturous, rapturous!

BALLADS FROM TIECK'S *MAGELONE* FOR VOICE AND PIANO, OP. 33
Dedicated to Julius Stockhausen;
Nos. 1–6 published 1865, Nos. 7–15 published 1868/9

[The full title of Tieck's 1796 prose tale with verse interludes is "Love Story of the Beautiful Magelone and Count Peter of Provence." A very brief synopsis will show how the 15 poems set by Brahms fit into the whole story. The young knight Peter is full of unformulated dreams until a wandering minstrel sings No. 1. Then Peter asks his parents to let him travel in search of adventure. His mother gives him three rings for his future bride. On leaving home, Peter sings No. 2, described as an "old song." In Naples, he and Magelone, the king's daughter, fall in love at a distance as he wins tourneys incognito. In his ardor he sings No. 3. He sends Magelone two of the rings, one with No. 4 and one with No. 5 in the form of written poems. Finally granted a personal meeting, he sings No. 6. At the tryst he presents the third ring and vows eternal fidelity; they kiss. Back in his lodging, he sings No. 7. Threatened with an unwanted bridegroom, Magelone asks Peter to run off with her to his homeland. Before meeting her he sings No. 8. In the course of their escape, they rest in a forest and he sings No. 9. A raven flies off with the three rings while Magelone sleeps and, trying to recover them when they fall into the sea, Peter is blown far from shore in a small boat; he sings No. 10. Magelone rides on sadly and goes to live in the hut of an old shepherd and his wife; she sings No. 11. Peter is found by Moors, who sell him to the Sultan; he sings No. 12. After nearly two years, Sulima, the Sultan's daughter, asks him to run away with her and he agrees, merely on the chance of reaching home again. Repenting, he sets out alone in a small boat as Sulima sings No. 13 in the distance. As his voyage gets under way, he sings No. 14. Eventually fishermen lead him to the shepherd's hut, where he discovers Magelone. Back in Provence, the three rings have been found by the royal cook in a fish's stomach. On every anniversary of their reunion, Peter and Magelone sing No. 15. Brahms omitted three of Tieck's poems, a nondramatic introductory one and two occurring between Nos. 14 and 15, no doubt because they would have seriously retarded the forward motion of his song cycle.—TRANSLATOR.]

1. No one has ever regretted mounting his steed to dash through the world in his lively youthful days. Mountains and meadows, lonely forest, maidens and ladies splendid in dress, golden jewelry—everything delights him with its beautiful form. Forms flee miraculously by, desires glow dreamily in his dazzled young mind, in his dazzled young mind. Fame swiftly strews roses in his path, love and caresses; laurel and roses lead him upward, lead him higher and higher upward. Round about him, joys, joys; succumbing, his enemies envy the hero, succumbing, envy the hero; then modestly he chooses the young woman who alone pleases him above all others, then modestly he chooses the young woman who alone pleases him above all others, above all others. And he wends his way back over mountains and fields and through lonely forests. His parents in tears, ah, all their longing—they are all united in charming happiness. After years have slipped by, he relates his adventures to his son in confidential moments, and shows him his wounds, the reward of bravery, of bravery. Thus even his old age remains young, even his old age, a beam of light, a beam of light in the dusk, a beam of light in the dusk.

2. Surely! bow and arrow are useful against the enemy; the weak-natured man weeps all the time in his helplessness, the weak-natured man weeps all the time in his helplessness. Health and happiness bloom for the noble man wherever the sun shines; the cliffs are steep but good fortune befriends him; but good fortune befriends him. Surely! bow and arrow are useful against the enemy; the weak-natured man weeps all the time in his helplessness, the weak-natured man weeps all the time in his helplessness. Health and happiness bloom for the noble man wherever the sun shines; the cliffs are steep but good fortune befriends him, good fortune befriends him. Surely! bow and arrow are useful against the enemy; the weak-natured man weeps all the time in his helplessness, the weak-natured man weeps all the time in his helplessness.

3. Are these pains, are these joys that are shooting through my heart? All my old desires depart, a thousand new flowers bloom. Through the twilight of my tears I see distant suns stand; what a yearning! what a longing! Do I dare? Shall I go closer? Ah, and when the teardrop falls, it is dark all around me; and yet no desire comes back to me, the future is devoid of hope. So beat, then, my ambitious heart; so flow down then, my tears. Ah, pleasure is only a deeper pain, life is a dark grave. Shall I endure this through no fault of my own? How is it that in my dreams my thoughts waver in every direction? I scarcely recognize myself. Shall I endure this through no fault of my own? How is it that in my dreams my thoughts waver in every direction, in every direction? I scarcely recognize myself. Oh, hear me, you kindly stars, oh, hear me, hear me, green meadow; you, O Love, hear my sacred oath, you, O Love, hear my sacred oath; if I remain far from her, I'll gladly die. Ah! ah! ah! only in the light, only in the light of her eyes dwell life and hope and happiness! If I remain far from her, I'll gladly die. Ah, only in the light, only in the light of her eyes, her eyes, dwell life and hope and happiness!

4. Love came from distant lands and no being followed her; and the goddess beckoned me, encircled me with delightful bonds, encircled me with delightful bonds. Then I began to feel pain; tears veiled my sight. "Alas, what is love's happiness?" I lamented, "to what purpose is this game, to what purpose is this game?" "I have found no one far and wide," the figure said sweetly; "now you must feel the power that used to bind people's hearts, that used to bind people's hearts." All my desires flew into the blue space of the sky; fame seemed like an idle dream to me, merely a roar of the ocean waves. Alas! who will now unloose my chains? For my arm is fettered; a swarm of cares flies about me; will no one, no one save me? May I look into the mirror that hope holds up to me? Ah, how deceptive the world is! No, I cannot trust it. Oh, but in spite of all, do not allow your only source of strength to falter; if the woman of your choice doesn't love you, only bitter death is left for the sick man, only bitter death is left for the sick man.

5. And so you are willing to show gracious mercy to the unfortunate man? And so it isn't a dream? How the fountains purl, how the waves murmur, how the trees rustle, how they rustle! I lay a prisoner deep in frightful castle walls; now the light greets me; how the beams play! They dazzle and illumine my timid face, my timid face. And shall I believe it? Will no one rob me of this precious delusion, this precious delusion? But dreams fade away, only loving is living: a welcome path, a welcome path! How free and how cheerful! Don't hasten any farther, away with your pilgrim's staff! You have overcome, you have found it, the most blessed, most blessed spot!

6. How am I then to bear the joy, the rapture, and keep my soul, my soul from departing as my heart pounds and pounds? And now, if the hours of love vanish, to what purpose is the desire to drag on a pleasureless life in a melancholy desert, if flowers blossom nowhere along the shore? How time passes with lead-weighted feet circumspectly step by step! And when I shall have to depart, how its foot will fly with feathery lightness, how its foot will fly with feathery lightness! Beat, force of my longing, deep in my faithful heart! Just as the note of a lute dies away, dies away, life's most beautiful pleasure flies off. Ah, how soon, ah, how soon I will scarcely be conscious of the bliss, the bliss, ah, how soon, ah, how soon I will scarcely be conscious of the bliss. Rush, rush on, deep current of time, you soon change yesterday to today, yesterday to today; you go from place, from place to place. If you have borne me up to now, sometimes merrily, sometimes quietly, I'll have the courage to continue—however, however it may turn out. Nevertheless, I shouldn't consider myself unfortunate, for the woman of my choice is beckoning to me; love won't let me perish of longing until my life comes to an end, until my life comes to an end! No, the stream becomes broader and broader, Heaven remains always cheerful to me; with a happy stroke of the oar I continue downstream, bringing love and life, love together with life, together, until the grave. No, the stream becomes broader and broader, Heaven remains always cheerful to me; with a happy stroke of the oar I continue downstream, with a happy stroke of the oar I continue downstream, bringing life together with love, until the grave, bringing life together with love, until the grave, bringing life together with love, until the grave, bringing life together with love, together, until the grave.

7. Was it you whose lips trembled, proffered for a sweet kiss? Does earthly life give such pleasure? Ha, how light, how light and splendor gleamed before my eyes, and all my senses strove toward those lips, all my senses strove toward those lips! In your clear eyes, longing flashed, beckoning to me tenderly, tenderly; everything, everything reverberated in my heart; I cast my eyes, my eyes down, and the breezes played songs of love; and the breezes played songs of love. Your eyes shone like a pair of stars, your golden hair cradled your face, your glance and smile took wing, and your sweet words roused my deepest longing; your glance and smile took wing, and your sweet words roused my deepest longing. Oh, the kiss, oh, the kiss—how burning red your lips were! I died, found life, life for the first time in that most beautiful death, in that most beautiful, most beautiful death.

8. We must be separated, beloved lute; it is time to race toward the far-off goal of my desire, the far-off goal of my desire. I am departing for the fray, for plunder, and after I obtain my booty I shall speed homeward. In the reddish glow I shall escape with her; my lance, my lance will protect us, my steel armor here, my lance, my steel armor here. Come, my dear weapons and armor, often worn for sport, now guard my happiness on this new path! I cast myself swiftly into the billows, I hail the splendid course; many a man before now was pulled in by the current, but the brave swimmer, the brave swimmer will keep his head above water. Ha! what pleasure to waste one's precious blood! To protect my joy, my priceless possession! When it comes to avoiding scorn, who lacks courage? When it comes to avoiding scorn, who lacks courage? Drop your reins, happy night! Open wide your wings, so that over the distant hills morning will soon smile upon us, morning, morning will soon smile upon us!

9. Rest, my darling, in the shade of the dusky green night; the grass in the meadows is whispering, the breeze fans and cools you, and true love stands guard. Sleep, fall asleep, the grove is rustling more softly; I am eternally yours, I am eternally, eternally yours. Be still, you hidden songsters, and do not disturb her sweet slumbers! The crowd of birds listens, their loud songs cease; close your eyes, beloved. Sleep, fall asleep, in the glow of twilight; I will guard you, I will guard you. Murmur on, you melodies; rush on, you quiet, quiet brook. Beautiful love fantasies speak in the melodies, gentle dreams float after them. Through the whispering grove, golden bees swarm and hum you to sleep, hum you, hum you to sleep.

10. Verzweiflung (Despair)

So resound, then, foaming waves, and curl yourselves about me, and curl yourselves about me! Let misfortune howl loudly around me, let misfortune howl loudly around me; let the cruel sea, the cruel sea be angry! I laugh at the raging storms, contemn the fury of the waters; oh, may I be smashed against the rocks!—for things will never, never again be good, for things will never again be good. I do not complain, even if I am now to be wrecked and to perish in the watery deep! My glance will never again be cheered at seeing the star of my love. So dash downward, [waves,] in the storms, and assail me, tempests, in your frenzy, and assail me, tempests, in your frenzy, so rocks crack against rocks, so rocks crack against rocks! I am a lost man, a lost man.

11. How soon light and splendor vanish; morning finds the wreath withered that gleamed in full glory yesterday, for it lost its bloom in the dark night. The wave of life floats by; even if it takes on bright colors, there is no profit, even if it takes on bright colors, there is no profit. The sun declines, the red glow flees; shadows lengthen and darkness spreads. Thus love floats away to desert lands; ah, if it could only last until the grave! But we awaken to deep sorrow: the boat breaks, the beam is extinguished; we are carried far off from the beautiful land to a barren shore where night surrounds us, to a barren shore where night surrounds us.

12. Must there be a separation that breaks the faithful heart? No, I don't call this living, even dying isn't this bitter. When I hear a shepherd's flute I suffer inward torment; when I gaze into the sunset, I think ardently of you. Does no true love exist, then? Must there, then, be pain, must there be pain and separation? If I had remained unloved, I would at least still have a ray of hope. But, as it is, I must now lament: where is hope except in the grave? I must take my misery far away; my heart is secretly breaking, my heart is secretly breaking.

13. SULIMA

Beloved man, where do your wandering feet now tarry? The nightingale babbles of longing and kisses, of longing and kisses. The trees are whispering in the golden glow, dreams are slipping into my window, into my window. Ah! do you know how my yearning heart is beating, how all my thoughts are full of sorrow and pleasure? Add wings to your haste and rescue me for your sake; under cover of night we will escape from here, under cover of night we will escape from here. The sails are billowing, fear [the correct German word is *Furcht*, not *Frucht*] is only a bauble: there, beyond the waves, is

your father's country, is your father's country. My homeland is vanishing—well, let it go! Love is drawing my mind on powerfully, my mind powerfully. Listen! the waves in the sea have a sensual sound; they are hopping and leaping wantonly around us, and should they complain? They are calling to you! They know they are carrying love away from here, they know they are carrying love away from here.

14. How gaily and vigorously my spirits rise; all fears are left behind. My heart is ambitious with new-found courage; a new, a new desire awakes. The stars are mirrored in the sea, and the waters have a golden glow, the waters have a golden glow. I dashed dizzily here and there and was neither bad nor good. But my doubts and the wavering of my thoughts are now dispelled; oh, carry me, you rocking waves, off to my long wished-for homeland. In the familiar, twilit distance—there songs of home are calling; from every star She looks down with gentle eyes, She looks down with gentle eyes. Become smooth, you faithful waves, lead me on distant paths to the dearly beloved threshold, finally, finally to meet my happiness, finally, finally to meet my happiness!

15. True love is long-lasting; it survives many, many an hour, and no despair frightens it; its courage is always staunch, its courage is always, always staunch. Even if storm and death threaten it with numerous armies, even if they strive to weaken its resolve, love counters the dangers with fidelity. And all that held the mind, the mind captive, is blown away like mist, and the wide world opens up to the happy springtime gaze, the wide, wide world opens up, opens up. Happiness is won, conquered by love; vanished the hours—they fly away—and blessed joy calms and fills the reeling, rapturously beating heart; let it be parted from pain forever, and never, and never, and never may lovely, blessed, heavenly joy, heavenly joy disappear, never disappear! Let it be parted from pain forever, and may blessed, heavenly joy never disappear! True love is long-lasting; may it be parted from pain, and may lovely, blessed, heavenly joy never disappear!

Johannes Brahms

COMPLETE SONGS FOR SOLO VOICE AND PIANO

SERIES I

Sechs Gesänge

für eine Tenor- oder Sopranstimme mit Pianofortebegleitung

Bettina von Arnim gewidmet

Johannes Brahms, Op. 3
(Veröffentlicht 1854)

1. Liebestreu

Rob. Reinick

Poco più mosso

„Und die Lieb, die du im Her . zen trägst, brich sie ab, brich sie ab, mein Kind!" Ob die Blum auch stirbt, wenn man sie bricht, treue Lieb nicht so ge - schwind.

„Und die Treu, und die Treu, 'swar

nur ein Wort, in den Wind da _ mit hin _ aus:" O

Mut _ ter, und split _ tert der Fels auch im Wind, mei _ ne Treu _ e, die hält ihn

aus, die hält, die

hält ihn aus.

2ᵃ Liebe und Frühling I

Hoffmann v. Fallersleben
(Ursprüngliche Fassung)

Wie sich Re-ben ran-ken schwingen in der lin-den Lüf-te Hauch,

wie sich wei-ße Win-den schlin-gen luf-tig um den Ro---sen-

strauch:_____ Al-so schmie-gen sich und ran-ken

früh-lings-se-lig, still und mild__ mei-ne Tag- und Nacht-ge-dan-ken

5

2ᵇ Liebe und Frühling I

Hoffmann v. Fallersleben
(Spätere Fassung)

Wie sich Re-ben ran-ken schwingen in der lin-den Lüf-te Hauch,

wie sich wei-ße Winden schlin-gen luf-tig um den Ro-sen

strauch: Al-so schmie-gen sich und ran-ken

früh-lings-se-lig, still und mild mei-ne Tag- und Nacht-ge-dan-ken

um ein trau - tes, lie - bes_ Bild,_____

Poco più lento

mei - ne Tag - und Nacht - ge -

dan - ken um ein_ trau - tes, lie - bes

Bild.

3. Liebe und Frühling II

Hoffmann v. Fallersleben

Ich will hin_aus, ich will_ zu dir,_ ich will_ es

selbst dir sa - gen: du bist mein Früh - ling, du_____ nur mir_____

in die - sen lich - - - - - - - - - ten

Ta - gen.

4. Lied

Aus dem Gedicht: „Ivan" von Bodenstedt

Ei _ ne Mö _ ve hoch ü _ ber der Wol _ ga fliegt, und Beu _ te spä _ hend im

Krei _ se sich wiegt. O hal _ te dich, Fischlein, im Was _ ser ver _ steckt, daß dich nicht die

spä _ hende Mö _ ve ent _ deckt! Und steigst du hin _ auf, so steigt sie her _ ab und macht dich zur

Beu _ te und führt dich zum Grab.

Ach, du grünende feuch_te Er_de du! Tu dich auf,___ leg mein stür_misches

Herz zur Ruh! Blaues Himmels_tuch mit der Stern_lein Zier, o trock_ne vom

Au_ge die Trä_ne mir! Hilf, Him_mel, der ar_men, der dul_denden Maid! Es bricht mir das

Herz, es bricht mir das Herz vor Weh und Leid,___ vor Weh und Leid!

5. In der Fremde

J. v. Eichendorff

mehr, kennt mich dort kei _ _ ner mehr. Wie

bald, ach wie bald kommt die stil _ le Zeit, da ru _ he ich auch und ü _ _ _

_ ber mir rauscht _ die schö _ ne Wald ein _ sam _ keit, und

kei _ ner kennt mich mehr hier, kei _ ner kennt mich mehr hier.

6. Lied

J. v. Eichendorff

Sechs Gesänge

für eine Sopran- oder Tenorstimme mit Begleitung des Pianoforte

Den Fräulein Luise und Minna Japha zugeeignet

Johannes Brahms, Op. 6
(Veröffentlicht 1853)

1. Spanisches Lied

Uebersetzt von P. Heyse

In dem Schatten mei — ner Lo — cken schlief mir mein Ge — lieb — ter ein; weck ich ihn nun auf? ___ Ach nein! Ach nein! Ach nein!

2 Pedale

Sorg‿lich strählt ich mei‿ne krau‿sen Lo‿cken täg‿‿lich in der Frü‿he,

doch umsonst ist mei‿ne Mü‿‿he, weil die Win‿de sie zer‿zau‿‿sen;

Lo‿ckenschatten, Win‿des‿sau‿sen

schlä‿fer‿ten den Lieb‿sten ein;

weck ich ihn nun auf? _____ Ach nein! Ach

nein! Ach nein! _____

Hö - ren muß ich, wie ihn grä - me, daß er schmachtet schon so lan - ge,

daß ihm Le - ben gäb und näh - me die - se mei - ne brau - ne

Wan - ge.

Und er nennt mich sei - ne Schlan - ge und doch schlief er bei mir ein;

weck ich ihn nun auf? ___ Ach

nein! Ach nein! Ach nein! ___

2 Pedale

2. Der Frühling

J. B. Rousseau

1. Es lockt und säu _ selt um den Baum: wach auf aus dei _ nem Schlaf und Traum, der Win _ ter ist _ zer _ ron _ nen, der Win _ ter ist _ zer _ ron _ nen. Da

2. Es zieht ein We _ hen sanft und lau, ge schau _ kelt in dem Wol _ ken bau wie Him _ mels _ duft _ her _ nie _ der, wie Him _ mels _ duft _ her _ nie _ der. Da

3. Es weht der Wind den Blü _ ten _ staub von Kelch zu Kelch, von Laub zu Laub, durch Ta _ ge und durch Näch _ te, durch Ta _ ge und _ durch Näch _ te. Flieg

schlägt er frisch den Blick em_por, die Au_gen se_hen hell her_vor ____
wer_den al _ le Blu_men wach, da tönt der Vö_gel schmelzend Ach, ____
auch, mein Herz, und flat_tre fort, such hier ein Herz und such es dort, ____

_ ans gold_ne Licht der Son _ nen,   ans __ gold_ne Licht der
_ da kehrt der Frühling wie _ der,   da __ kehrt der Früh_ling
_ du triffst vielleicht das Rech _ te,   du __ triffst vielleicht das

Son _ _ nen.
wie _ _ der.
Rech _ te.

3. Nachwirkung

Alfred Meissner

So hän-gen noch lang ___ nach dem Scheiden des

Ta _ ges in säuselnder Nacht-luft, beim säuselnden Win _ de die Bienen wie trun-ken und won-ne-ver-

sun _ _ ken an zit-tern-den Blü _ ten der duf-ti-gen Lin _ de, an

zit _ tern _ den Blü _ ten der duf-ti _ gen Lin _ _ _ de.

4. Juchhe

R. Reinick

sin‿gen so fröh‿li‿che Lie‿der, und sin‿gen, und sin‿gen,
ma‿len im kla‿ren Spie‿gel die Gär‿ten und Hü‿gel,

in den blau‿en Him‿mel hin‿ein, in den Him‿mel hin‿ein,
und die Wol‿ken, die drü‿ber gehn, die drü‿ber gehn,

in den blau‿en Him‿mel hin‿ein.
und die Wol‿ken, die drü‿ber gehn!

2. Wie
3. Und

5. Wie die Wolke nach der Sonne

Hoffmann v. Fallersleben

und berauscht vom Son _ nen _ ba _ de blind zur Er _ de nie _ _ _ der _

fällt: So auch muß ich schmach _ ten, ban _ gen,

spähn und trach _ ten, dich zu sehn, will an dei _ nen Bli _ cken han _ gen,

und an ih _ rem Glanz ver _ gehn, und _____ an

ih _ rem Glanz ver _ gehn, _____ ver _ _ gehn.

6. Nachtigallen schwingen

Hoffmann v. Fallersleben

Nach _ ti _ gal _ len schwin _ gen

lu _ stig ihr Ge _ fie _ _ der, Nach _ ti _ gal _ len sin _ gen

ih _ re al _ ten Lie _ der. Und die Blu _ men

al _ le, sie er _ wa _ chen wie _ der bei dem Klang und

Schal — le al — ler die — ser Lie — — — — — der.

Und mei — — ne Sehn — sucht wird zur Nach — ti — gall und fliegt in die blü — hen — de

Welt hin — ein, und fragt bei den Blu — men ü — — ber — all,

wo mag doch mein, mein Blüm_chen sein? wo mein

Blüm _ chen sein?

Und die Nach_ti_gal_len

schwin_gen ih _ ren Rei _ gen un _ ter Lau_bes_hal_len

zwi _ schen Blü _ ten _ zwei _ gen, von den Blu _ men

al _ len a _ ber ich muß schwei _ gen. Un _ _ ter ih _ _ nen

steh ich trau _ rig sin _ nend still:

Ei _ ne Blu _ me seh ich, die nicht blü _ hen will.

Sechs Gesänge

für eine Singstimme mit Begleitung des Pianoforte

Albert Dietrich gewidmet

Johannes Brahms, Op. 7
(Veröffentlicht 1854)

1. Treue Liebe

Eduard Ferrand

kämst du, mein Lieb‿ster, doch heu‿ ‿te, ach, kämst du, mein Lieb‿ster, doch
find ich, mein Lieb‿ster, dich wie‿ ‿der, wo find ich, mein Lieb‿ster, dich

heu ‿ ‿ ‿ te!" Die
wie ‿ ‿ ‿ der?"

sempre Ped.

Was ‿ ser um‿spiel‿ten ihr schmeichelnd den Fuß, wie Träu ‿ me von se ‿ li ‿ gen

Stun ‿ den, es zog sie zur Tie ‿ fe mit stil ‿ ‿ ‿ ler Ge‿

walt;_____ nie

stand mehr am U_fer die hol_de Ge_stalt, sie hat den Ge_lieb_ten ge_

fun_____den!_____

2. Parole

J. v. Eichendorff

stand wohl am Fen _ ster _ bo _ _ gen und flocht sich trau _ rig das Haar, der
als der Frühling ge _ kom _ men, die Welt war von Blü _ ten ver _ schneit, da

Jä _ ger war fort _ ge _ zo _ gen, der Jä _ ger ihr Lieb _ ster war.
hat sie ein Herz sich ge _ nom _ men, und ging in die grü _ ne Haid.

Und

Sie

legt___ das Ohr an den Ra___sen, hört fer___ner Hu___fe
A___bends die Wäl___der rau___schen, von fern nur fällt noch ein

Klang, das sind___ die Re___he, die gra___sen am
Schuß, da steht___ sie stil___le zu lau___schen: „das

schat___ti___gen Ber___ges___hang, am schat___ti___gen Ber___ges___
war meines Lieb___sten Gruß! das war meines Lieb___sten

dim. poco rit.

1. **2.**

hang. Und Gruß!" Da

3. Anklänge

J. v. Eichendorff

Hoch ü — ber stil — len Hö — hen stand in dem Wald ein Haus; so ein — sam wars zu se — — hen dort ü — bern Wald hin — aus. Ein

Mäd_chen saß dar_in_ _ _nen bei stil_ _ler A_bend_zeit,

tät seid_ne Fä_den spin_ _nen zu ih_rem Hoch_zeits_

kleid, tät seid_ne Fä_den spin_ _nen zu

ih_ _ rem Hoch_zeits_kleid.

4. Volkslied

5. Die Trauernde

Volkslied

Mei Mue_ter mag mi net, und kei Schatz han i net,
Ge_stern isch Kirchweih g'wä, mi hot mer g'wis net g'seh,

ei wa_rum sterb i net, was tu i do?
denn mir ischs gar so weh, i tanz ja net. Laßt die drei Ro_se stehn,

die an dem Kreuzle blühn: hent ihr das Mädle kennt, die drun_ter liegt?

6. Heimkehr

L. Uhland

O brich nicht, Steg, du zit_terst sehr, o stürz nicht, Fels, du dräu_est schwer; Welt, geh nicht un_ter,

Lieder und Romanzen

für eine Singstimme mit Begleitung des Pianoforte

Johannes Brahms, Op. 14
(Veröffentlicht 1861)

1. Vor dem Fenster

Volkslied

lein, a - de, a - de, es muß ge - schie - den sein.

Ach Schei - den, Schei - den ü - ber Schei - den, Scheiden tut

mei - nem jun - gen Her - zen weh, _____ daß ich mein schön Herz - lieb muß mei - den,

das ver - geß ich nim - mer - mehr. _____

2. Vom verwundeten Knaben
Volkslied

1. Es wollt ein Mäd-chen früh auf - stehn   und in den
2. als sie nun in den grü-nen Wald kam,   da fand sie
3. Knab, der war von Blut so rot,   und als sie

grü - nen Wald spa - zie - ren gehn.＿＿＿   2. Und
ei - nen ver - wund'- ten Knab'n.＿＿＿   3. Der
sich ver - wandt, war er schon tot.＿＿＿

4. Wo krieg ich nun zwei Leid - fräu - lein, die mein feins Lieb zu

Gra - be wein'n? Wo krieg ich nun sechs Reu - ter - knab'n, die

mein feins Lieb zu Gra_be trag'n? Wie lang soll ich denn

trau_ern gehn? Bis al_le Was_ser zu_sam_men

gehn?_____ Ja al_le Was_ser gehn nicht zu_sam'n, so

wird mein Trau_ern kein En_de han._____

3. Murrays Ermordung

Schottisch; aus Herders Stimmen der Völker

3. Ein schö-ner Rit-ter war er, in
4. schö-ner Rit-ter war er, bei

Wett = und Rin-ge-Lauf; all-zeit war uns-res Mur-ray die Kro-ne o-ben
Waf-fen-spiel und Ball; es war der ed-le Mur-ray die Blu-me ü-ber-

più f   *più f ancora*

drauf.
all.

4. Ein schö-ner Rit-ter war er, in Tanz und Sai-ten-

5. Ein

spiel; ach, daß der ed-le Mur-ray der Kö-ni-gin ge-fiel.

O Kö - ni - gin, wirst lan - ge sehn ü - ber Schlos - ses

Wall, eh du den schö - nen Mur - ray siehst rei - ten in dem

Tal, siehst rei - ten in dem Tal.

4. Ein Sonett

Aus dem 13. Jahrhundert

Langsam, sehr innig

Ach könnt ich, könn_te ver_ges_sen sie, ihr schö_nes,

lie_bes, lieb_li_ches We_sen, den Blick, die freund_li_che Lip_pe

die! Viel_leicht ich möch_te ge_ne_sen! Doch ach, mein Herz, mein

Poco più animato

Herz kann es nie! Und doch ists Wahnsinn, zu hof_fen sie! Und

um _ sie schweben, gibt Mut _ und Le _ ben, zu wei _ chen nie. _ _

rit. _ _ _ p Tempo I

Und denn, wie kann ich ver _ ges _ sen sie, ihr schö _ nes,

lie _ bes, lieb _ li _ ches We _ sen, den Blick, die freund _ li _ che Lip _ pe die? Viel

lie _ ber nim _ mer ge _ ne _ _ _ sen!

Thibault; deutsch von Herder.

5. Trennung

Volkslied

1. Wach auf, wach auf, du junger Gesell, du hast so lang geschlafen, da drau_ßen sin_gen die Vö_gel hell, der Fuhr_mann lärmt auf der

2. auf, wach auf, mit hel_ler Stimm hub an der Wäch_ter zu ru_fen, wo zwei Herz_lie_ben bei_sam_men sind, da müs_sen sie sein gar

3. Kna_be war ver_schla_fen gar, er schlief so lang, so sü_ße, die Jung_frau a_ber wei_se war, weckt ihn durch ih_re

Stra _ _ ßen!
klu _ _ ge.
Küs _ _ se!

f 2. Wach
p 3. Der

4. Das Schei - den, Schei - den tu - et not, wie

Tod ist es so har - te, der scheid't auch man - ches

Münd - lein rot und man - che Buh - len zar - - - te.

5. Der Kna - be auf sein

Röß - lein sprang und trab - te schnell von dan - nen, die

Jung - frau sah ihm lan - ge nach, groß Leid tat sie um -

fan - gen!

6. Gang zur Liebsten

Volkslied

1. Des A - bends kann ich nicht schla - fen gehn, zu mei-ner Herz-lieb - sten
2. Wer ist denn da? wer klop - fet an, der mich so leis auf-
3. Wenn al - le Ster - ne Schrei - ber gut, und al - le Wol-ken Pa -
4. Ach hätt ich Fe - dern wie ein Hahn und könnt ich schwim-men

muß ich gehn, zu mei-ner Herz-lieb - sten muß ich gehn, und sollt ich an der
we - cken kann? Das ist der Herz-al - ler - lieb - ste dein, steh auf, mein Schatz, und
pier da - zu, so soll - ten sie schrei-ben der Lie - ben mein, sie brächten die Lieb in den
wie ein Schwan, so wollt ich schwimmen wohl ü - ber den Rhein, hin zu der Herz-al - ler-

Tür blei-ben stehn, ganz hei - - me - lig!
laß mich ein, ganz hei - - me - lig!
Brief nicht ein, ganz hei - - me - lig!
lieb - sten mein, ganz hei - - me - lig!

7. Ständchen

Volkslied

hü - ten all, die in dem Him - mel sind! Gut Nacht, gut
schla - fen tu, mein Herz um dich doch wacht; daß es in
Fen - ster dir, guckt in dein Käm - mer - lein; der Mond schaut

Nacht, mein lie - ber Schatz, schlaf du, schlaf du von nach - ten lind,
lau - ter Lie - bes - glut an dich, an dich der Zeit ge - dacht,
dich im Schlum - mer da, doch ich, doch ich muß ziehn al - lein,

schlaf du _____ von nach - ten lind!
an dich _____ der Zeit ge - dacht.
doch ich _____ muß ziehn al - lein!

p

1. 2.   3.

2. Schlaf
3. Es

8. Sehnsucht
Volkslied

Mein Schatz ist nicht da, ist weit ü-berm See, und so oft ich dran

denk, tut mirs Her-ze so weh! Schön blau ist der See und mein Herz tut mir weh, und mein

Herz wird nicht g'sund, bis mein Schatz wie-der kommt! Schön blau ist der See und mein

Herz tut mir weh, und mein Herz wird nicht g'sund, bis mein Schatz wie-der kommt.

Fünf Gedichte

für eine Singstimme mit Begleitung des Pianoforte

Johannes Brahms, Op. 19
(Veröffentlicht 1862)

1. Der Kuß

Hölty

Zu_ckend fliegt nun der Kuß, wie ein ver_sen_gend Feur,

mir durch Mark und Ge_bein. Du, die Un_sterb_lich_

keit durch die Lip_pen mir sprüh_te, we_he, we_he mir Küh_lung zu,

Küh_ _ _lung zu!

2. Scheiden und Meiden

L. Uhland

Nicht zu langsam und mit starkem Ausdruck

So soll ich dich nun mei _ den, du mei _ nes
Lieb _ chen, heißt das mei _ den, wenn man sich

Le _ bens Lust! Du küs _ sest mich zum Schei _
herzt und küßt? Ach, Lieb _ chen, heißt das schei _

den, ich drü _ cke dich an die Brust!
den, wenn man sich fest __ um _ schließt?

Ach,

3. In der Ferne

L. Uhland

Will ru _ hen un _ ter den Bäu _ men hier, die Vög _ lein

hör ich so ger _ ne. Wie

sin _ get ihr so _ zum Her _ zen mir, wie singt ihr zum Her _ zen mir?

Von un _ srer Lie _ be was wis _ set ihr in die _ ser wei _ ten

Fer _ ne, in die _ ser wei _ ten Fer _ ne?

Will ru _ hen hier an des Ba _ ches Rand, wo duf _ ti _ ge

Blüm _ lein sprie _ _ ßen. Wer hat _ euch

Blüm _ lein hie _ her _ ge _ sandt? wer hat euch hie _ her _ ge _

4. Der Schmied

L. Uhland

5. An eine Aeolsharfe

Mörike

_di_ _sche Kla_ _ _ _ge.   Ihr

kom _ met, Win _ de, fern her _ ü _ ber,   ach, von des Kna _ ben,

der mir so lieb war,   frisch grü _ nen_dem Hü _ gel.   Und

Früh _ lings_blü _ _ _ten un_ter_we_ges strei _ fend   ü _ ber_

süßem Er schre cken meiner See le plötz li che

Poco più lento

Re gung, und hier die vol le Ro se

streut ge schüt telt all ih re Blät ter vor mei ne

Fü ße.

dim.

Lieder und Gesänge

von Aug. v. Platen und G.F. Daumer

für eine Singstimme mit Begleitung des Pianoforte

Johannes Brahms, Op.32
(Veröffentlicht 1864)

1

Wie rafft ich mich auf in der Nacht, in der Nacht, und fühl_te mich für_der, mich für_der ge_zo_gen, fühl_te mich für_der ge_zo_gen, die Gas_sen ver_ließ ich vom

Wäch_ter be_wacht, durch_wan_del_te sacht in der Nacht, in der Nacht das

Tor mit dem go_thischen Bo _ _ _ _ _ gen.

Der

Mühl_bach rausch_te durch fel_si_gen Schacht, ich lehn_te mich ü_ber die

we - he, wie hast du die Ta - ge ver - bracht, nun

stil - le du sacht in der Nacht, in der Nacht, im po - chenden Her - zen die

Reu - - - - e!   Aug. v. Platen

2

Nicht mehr zu dir zu ge-hen, be-schloß ich und beschwor ich,

und ge-he je-den A-bend, denn je-de Kraft, denn je-de

Kraft und je-den Halt ver-lor ich.

espress. animato

Ich möch_te nicht mehr le _ ben, möcht Au _ gen _ blicks, Au _ gen_blicks ver _

animato

der _ _ ben, und möch _ te doch_ auch_ le _ ben für dich, mit

dir, und nim _ _ mer, nim _ _ mer ster _ _ _ ben.

poco riten.

Tempo I

Ach re_de, sprich ein Wort nur, ein ein_zi_ges, ein kla_res;

gib Le_ben o_der Tod mir, nur dein Ge_fühl,— nur dein Ge_

fühl_ enthül_le mir, dein wah_res! G. F. Daumer. Aus der Moldau

3

Singstimme

Pianoforte

Mäßig

Ich schleich um_her be_trübt und stumm, du fragst, o fra_ge mich
Der Baum ver_dorrt, der Duft ver_geht, die Blät_ter lie_gen so

nicht wa_rum?
gelb im Beet,

Das Herz er_schüt_tert
es stürmt ein Schau_er

so man_che Pein!
mit Macht her_ein,

und könnt ich je___ zu dü_ster
und könnt ich je___ zu dü_ster

sein,
sein,

zu dü_ster sein?
zu dü_ster sein? Aug. v. Platen

4

ist die Ro - se, die die Freun - din am Her - zen trug, und

je - ner Kuß, der mich be - rausch - te, wo ist, wo ist, wo

ist er nun? Und

Più agitato

je - ner Mensch, der ich ge - we - sen, und den ich längst mit

ei - - nem an - dern Ich ver - tausch - te, wo

ist, wo ist, wo ist er nun?

wo ist er

nun? Aug. v. Platen

5

We _ he, so willst du mich wie _ der, hemmen_de Fes _ sel, um _ fan _ gen? Auf _ _ _ und hin _ aus _ _ _ in die Luft,

Stre _ be demWind nur ent _ ge _ gen, daß er die Wan _ ge dir küh _ le, _ ße den Him _ mel mit Lust,

auf _ _ _ und hin _ aus, _ _ _ und hin _
grü _ _ ße den Him _ mel, den

col 8va ad lib.

mf

cresc.

sau - - - - - gend, sau - - - - gend ä -
at - - - - - me, at - - - - me den

the - - - - - - ri - schen Duft!
Feind _____ aus der Brust! Aug. v. Platen

6

sprichst, daß ich mich täusch‿te, be‿schworst es hoch und hehr, ich

weiß ja doch, du lieb‿test, al‿lein du liebst nicht mehr, du liebst, du

liebst nicht mehr!

Dein schö_nes Au_ge brann_te, die Küs_se brann_ten sehr, du lieb_test mich, be_kenn es, al_lein du liebst nicht mehr, du liebst, du liebst nicht mehr!

dolce

cresc.

f

p

Ich

zäh - le nicht auf neu - e, ge - treu - e Wie - der -

kehr: Ge - steh nur, daß du lieb - test, und

lie - be mich nicht mehr, _____ und lie _ _ be,

lie _ _ be mich nicht mehr! _____ Aug. v. Platen

7

wer _ den all zu rei _ nen Gna _ den,

denn sie müs _ sen, um zu scha _ den, schif _ fen ü _ ber ei _ ne Lip _ pe,

die die Sü _ ße sel _ ber ist, die die Sü _ ße sel _ ber

ist.   G. F. Daumer, nach Hafis

8

In gehender Bewegung

Singstimme

So stehn wir, ich und meine Weide, so leider
mit ein an der Bei de: Nie kann ich
ihr was tun zu Lie be, nie kann sie mir was tun zu
Lei de.

Pianoforte

Sie krän_ket es, wenn ich die Stirn ihr mit ei_nem Di _ a_

dem be _ klei _ de;

Ich dan _ ke selbst, wie für ein Lä _ cheln der

Huld, für ih _ re Zorn _ be _ schei _ de.

So stehn wir, ich und meine Wei_de, so lei_der mit ein_an_der

Bei_de, so lei_der mit ein_an_der Bei___

de. G. F. Daumer, nach Hafis

9

espress.

Laß mich ver - gehn in deinem Arm! Es ist in ihm ja selbst der Tod,— ob auch die herb - ste To - des - qual die Brust durch - wü - te, won - ne - voll, won - ne - won - ne - voll!

G. F. Daumer, nach Hafis

Ped.

Romanzen
aus L. Tiecks Magelone
für eine Singstimme mit Pianoforte

Julius Stockhausen gewidmet

Johannes Brahms, Op. 33
(Nr. 1–6 veröffentlicht 1865, Nr.7–15 1868/69)

1

Kei - nen hat es noch ge-reut, der das Roß be-stie - gen, um in fri - scher Ju - gend-zeit durch die Welt zu flie - gen.

Ber - ge und Au - en, ein - samer Wald, Mäd - chen und Frau - en

dim.

p

poco a poco cresc.

präch - tig im Klei - de, gol - den Ge - schmei - de, al - les er -

freut _____ ihn mit schö - ner Ge - stalt.

p

Wun _ derlich   flie _ hen Ge _ stal _ ten da _ hin, _____

schwär-merisch   glü _ hen   Wün _ _ _ sche   in   ju _ gendlich   trun _ kenem

Sinn,   in   ju _ gendlich   trun _ kenem   Sinn.

gend, den Held, be - nei - den, er - lie - gend, den

Held, — dann wählt er be - schei - den das

Fräu - lein, das ihm nur vor al - len ge - fällt,

dann wählt er be - schei - den das Fräu - lein, das ihm nur vor

al - len, vor al - len ge - fällt.

Und Ber - - - ge und Fel - der und

ein - sa - me Wäl - der mißt er zu - rück.

Die El - tern in Trä - nen, ach al - le ihr

Seh - nen,— sie al - le ver - ei - nigt das lieb -

lich - ste Glück.

Sind Jah -

re ver - schwun - den, er - zählt er dem Sohn in

trau - li - chen Stun - den, und zeigt __ sei - ne Wun - den,

der Tap - fer - keit, der Tap - - - ferkeit Lohn.

So bleibt das Al - ter, das Al - ter selbst noch jung,

ein Licht - strahl, ein Licht - - strahl in __ der __

Däm - me - rung, ein Licht - strahl in

der Däm - - - - - me - rung.

2

Traun! Bo - gen und Pfeil sind gut für den Feind, hülf -

los al - le - weil der E - len - de weint, hülf los al - le -

weil __ der E - len - de weint;

dem Ed - len blüht Heil, wo Son - ne nur scheint, die

Fel - sen sind steil, doch Glück ist sein Freund, doch Glück ist sein Freund.

Traun! Bo - gen und Pfeil sind gut für den Feind, hülf - los al - le -

weil der E - len - de weint, hülf - los al - le - weil der E - len - de

weint;   dem

Ed_len blüht Heil, wo Son_ne nur scheint, die Fel_sen sind steil, doch Glück ist sein Freund, doch

Glück ist sein Freund. Traun! Bo _ gen und Pfeil sind gut für den

Feind, hülf _ los al _ le _ weil der E _ len _ de weint, hülf _ los al _ le _

weil der E _ len _ de weint.

3

1. Sind es Schmer _ zen, sind___ es Freu _ den,   die durch
2. Durch die Däm _ me _ rung___ der Trä _ nen   seh ich

mei _ nen Bu _ sen ziehn?___   Al _ le al _ ten Wün _ sche
fer _ ne Son _ nen stehn,___   welches Schmach _ ten! wel _ ches

Zu - kunft ist von Hoff - nung leer. So

schla - ge denn, stre - ben des Herz, so flie - ßet denn, Trä - nen, her - ab,

ach, Lust ist nur tie - fe - rer Schmerz,

Le - ben ist dunk - les Grab.

Vivace

Oh - ne Verschul - den soll ich er - dul - den? Wie ist's, daß mir im Traum al - le Ge - dan - ken auf und nie - derschwanken! Ich ken - ne mich noch kaum. Oh - ne Ver-schul - den soll ich er - dul - den? Wie ist's, daß mir im Traum al - le Ge - dan - ken auf und nie - der, auf und

niederschwanken! Ich kenne mich noch kaum.

Vivace

O hört mich, ihr gütigen Sterne,

o höre mich, höre mich, grünende

Flur, du, Liebe, den

Hoff-nung und Glück!

p

Bleib ich ihr fer _ ne,

cresc.

sterb ich ger _ ne.

f

Ach! nur_ im Licht, nur im Licht von_

ih _ rem, von ih _ rem_ Blick wohnt Le _ _ _ ben und Hoff _ nung und

ad libit.

Glück!

a tempo

f

f

4

Ach! was ist_ der Lie_be_ Glück, klagt ich, wo_zu die_ses Spie_

len, wo_zu die_ses Spie_ _len?

Kei_nen hab ich weit ge_fun_den, sag_te_ lieb_lich die_ Ge_stalt,

füh_le du nun die Ge_walt, die die Her_zen sonst gebun_den,

die die Her_zen sonst ge _ bun_den.

Poco vivace e sempre animato

Al _ _ le mei_ne Wünsche flo _ gen

cresc. ed animato

in der Lüf_te blauen Raum, Ruhm schien mir ein

Mor _ _ gen_traum, nur ein Klang der Mee _ res_wo_gen.

Darf ich in den Spiegel schau _ en, den die Hoffnung vor mir hält? Ach, wie trü _ gend ist die Welt! Nein, ich kann ihr nicht ver_ trau _ en.

Tempo I

O, und den_noch laß nicht wan_ken, was dir_ nur noch Stär_ke_ gibt,

wenn die Einz_ge dich nicht liebt,_ bleibt nur bitt_rer Tod dem Kran_ken,

bleibt nur_ bitt_rer_ Tod dem Kran_ken.

5

Allegro

Singstimme

So willst du des Ar _ men dich

Pianoforte

gnä _ dig er _ bar _ men? So ist es kein Traum?

Wie rie _ seln die Quellen, wie tö _ _ nen die Wel _ len, wie

rau _ _ _ _ _ schet, wie rau _ _ _ _ _ schet der Baum!

Tief lag ich in ban-gen Ge-mäu-ern ge-fan-gen, nun grüßt_____ mich das Licht, wie spie-len die Strahlen! sie blen-den und ma-len mein schüch-_-tern Ge-sicht, mein schüch-_-_-tern Ge-sicht.

Und soll ich es glauben? Wird kei _ ner mir

rau _ ben den köst _ _ li _ chen Wahn, den köst _

_ li _ chen Wahn? Doch Träu _ me ent _ schweben, nur lie _ ben heißt

le _ ben: Will _ kom _ me _ ne Bahn, will _ kom _ _ me _ _ ne Bahn!

6

Wie soll ich die Freu _ de, die Won _ ne denn tra _ gen? Daß

un _ ter dem Schlagen, dem Schla _ gen des Her _ zens die See _ le, die See _ le nicht

schei _ de?

Und wenn nun die Stun _ den der

Lie _ be ver_schwunden, wo _ zu das Ge _ lü _ ste, in trau _ ri_ger Wü _ ste noch

wei _ ter ein lust _ lee_res Le _ ben zu ziehn, wenn nir _ gend dem U _ fer mehr

Blu _ _ men er _ _ blühn? Wie

geht mit blei _ behang _ nen Fü _ ßen die Zeit bedäch _ tig Schritt vor

Schritt! Und wenn ich wer _ _ de schei _ den _ müs _ sen, wie

fe _ der _ leicht fliegt dann ihr Tritt, wie fe _ der _ leicht fliegt

poco ritard. _ _ _ _ Poco sostenuto

dann _ ihr Tritt!

Won_ne mir kaum noch be_ _wußt.

p dimin.

Rausche, rau _ sche wei_ter fort, tie _ _fer Strom_ der

p

Zeit, wandelst bald aus Morgen Heut, aus Morgen Heut,

gehst_ von Ort,_ von Ort zu Ort; hast du

dolce

mich bisher ge - tra - gen, lu - stig bald, dann

still, will es nun auch wei - ter wa - gen, wie___ es,

wie___ es wer - den will.

Poco animato

Darf mich doch nicht e _ _ lend ach _ ten,

da die Einz _ _ ge winkt, Lie _ _ be läßt mich

nicht verschmach _ ten, bis dies Le _ ben sinkt,

bis dies Le _ ben sinkt!

fahr_____ ich hin _ ab, bring Lie _

_ _ be und Le _ ben, Lie _ be und Le _ ben zu _ gleich, zu _

gleich an das Grab.

Nein, der Strom wird im _ _ _ mer brei _ ter,_____

7

streb - ten, al - le Sin - ne nach den Lip _ _ _ pen

streb _ ten! In den kla _ ren Au _ gen blink _ te

Sehn _ sucht; die mir zärt _ lich, zärt _ lich wink _ te,

al _ les, al _ les klang im Her _ zen

wie - der, mei - ne Bli - cke, mei - ne Bli - cke san -

- ken nie - der, und die Lüf - te tön - ten Lie - bes -

lie - der, und _ die Lüf - te tön _ ten Lie - - - bes -

lie - der.

Animato

Wie ein Ster-nenpaar glänzten die Augen, die Wan-gen wieg-ten das gol-de-ne Haar,

pp

Blick und Lä-cheln schwan-gen Flü-gel und die sü-ßen Wor-te gar weck-ten das

tiefste Ver-lan - - -gen; Blick und Lä-cheln schwan-gen

Flü-gel und die sü-ßen Wor-te gar weckten das tiefste Ver-lan - gen;

O Kuß,_____ o Kuß, wie war dein Mund so

bren _ nend rot! Da starb ich, fand ein Le _ ben, ein Le _ ben

erst im schön _ sten Tod, im schön _ sten, schön _ _ _ sten

Tod.

8

zie - he zum Strei - te, zum Rau - be hinaus, und hab ich die Beu - te, dann

flieg ich nach Haus. Im röt - li chen Glan - ze ent-

flieh ich mit ihr, es schützt uns die Lan - ze, die Lan - ze, der Stahl - harnisch

hier, die Lan - ze, der Stahl - har - nisch hier.

Allegro

Kommt, lie _ be Waf _ fen _ stü _ cke, zum Scherz oft an _ ge _

tan, be _ schir _ met jetzt mein Glü _ cke auf die _ ser neu _ en Bahn!

Ich wer _ fe mich rasch in die Wo _ gen, ich

grü _ ße den herr _ li _ chen Lauf, __ schon man _ cher ward

niе - der - ge - zo - gen, der tap - fe - re Schwim - mer, der tap - fe - re

Schwim - mer bleibt o - ben auf. Ha!

Lust zu ver - geu - den das e - de - le Blut! Zu schü - tzen die

Freu - de, mein köst - li - ches Gut! Nicht

Hohn zu er - lei - den, wem fehlt es an Mut? Nicht

Hohn zu er - lei - den, wem fehlt es an Mut?

dimin. e ritard. molto

pp

Andante

Sen - ke die Zü - gel, glück - li - che Nacht!

p

Span _ ne die Flü _ gel, daß ü _ ber fer _ ne Hü _ _ _

gel uns schon der Mor _ _ gen lacht, uns _____

_____ schon der Mor _ gen, der Mor _ _ _ _ _ gen _____

lacht!

cresc.

p dolce

Ped.

9

wacht. Schla - fe, schlaf ein,

lei - ser rauscht der Hain, e - wig bin ich

dein, e - wig, e - wig bin ich dein.

Schweigt, ihr ver _ steck _ ten Ge _ sän _ _ _ ge, und stört nicht die sü _ ße _ ste

p dolce

Ruh! Es lauscht der Vö _ gel Ge _ drän _ ge, es

ru _ hen die lau _ ten Ge _ sän _ ge, schließ, Lieb _ chen, dein

dolce

Au _ _ ge zu. Schla _ _ fe, schlaf

p

ein, im däm _ _ mern _ den Schein,

ich will dein Wäch _ ter sein, ich will dein

Wäch _ _ _ ter sein.

und sum _ _ men zum Schlum _ _ mer dich

ein, sum _ _ _ men zum Schlum _ mer, zum Schlum _

dimin. pp

_ _ mer dich ein.

p dim.

sempre e poco ritard. pp

10

Verzweiflung

So tö _ _ net denn, schäu _ men de Wel _ len,

und win _ _ det euch rund _____ um mich her, und

win _ _ det euch rund _____ um mich her! Mag

mö _ gen mich Fel _ sen zer _ schmet _ tern! denn nim _ mer, denn

nim _ _ mer wird es gut, denn nim _ _ mer wird es

gut.

un poco ritard.

sostenuto

Ossia:

dimin.

So wälzt _____ euch berg ab _____ mit Ge _ wit _ tern, und ra _ _ _ set, ihr Stür _ _ me, mich an, und

ra _ _ _ set, ihr Stür _ _ me, mich an, daß

Fel _ sen an Fel_sen zer_split_tern, daß Fel _ sen an Fel_sen zer_split_tern!

Ich bin ein ver_lo _ _ re_ner Mann, ein ver_lo _ _ re _ ner

Mann.

11

Etwas langsam

Singstimme

Pianoforte

p *espress.*

Wie schnell ver_schwin_det so Licht als_ Glanz, der

Mor_gen fin_det ver_welkt_ den Kranz, der ge_stern glüh_te in

al_ler Pracht, denn er_ ver_blüh_te in dunk_ler Nacht.

Es schwimmt die Wel _ le des Le _ bens hin, und

färbt sich hel _ le, hats nicht Ge _ winn, und färbt sich hel _ le, hats

nicht Ge _ winn; die

Son ne nei _ get, die Rö _ te flieht, der

Schat _ ten stei _ get und Dun _ kel zieht.

So schwimmt die Lie _ be zu

Wü _ sten ab, ach, daß ___ sie blie _ be bis an ___ das

Grab! Doch wir ___ er _ wa _ chen zu tie _ fer Qual: es

bricht __ der Na_chen, es löscht __ der Strahl,

vom schö_nen Lan_de weit weg __ ge_bracht zum

ö _ den Stran_de, wo um __ uns Nacht, zum ö _ den Stran_de, wo

um __ uns Nacht.

12

Poco Andante

Muß _____ es ei _ ne Tren _ nung
Hör _____ ich ei _ nes Schä _ fers

ge _ ben, die _____ das treu _ e Herz _ zer _ bricht?
Flö _ te, här _ _ _ me ich mich in _ nig _ lich,

Nein, _____ dies nen _ ne ich nicht le _ _ ben, ster _ _ ben
seh _____ ich in die A _ bend _ rö _ _ te, denk _____ ich

ist so bit _ ter nicht.
brün _ stig _ lich an dich.

Gibt _____ es denn kein wah _ res Lie _ ben? muß denn

Schmerz, _____ muß denn Schmerz und Tren _ nung sein? Wär ich

un _ ge _ liebt ge _ blie _ ben, hätt ich doch noch Hoff _ nungsschein.

A _ _ ber so muß ich nun kla _ gen: wo _____ ist

Hoff - nung, als — das Grab? Fern ——— muß ich — mein E - lend

tra - gen, heim - - lich bricht das Herz — mir

sempre poco ritard.

ab, heim - - lich bricht das Herz — mir

sempre poco ritard. e dimin.

ab.

13

Sulima

Ge _ lieb _ ter, wo zau _ dert dein
flü _ stern die Bäu _ me im

ir _ 'ren _ der Fuß? die Nach _ ti _ gall plau _ dert von Sehn _ sucht und
gol _ de _ nen Schein, es schlüp _ fen mir Träu _ me zum Fen _ ster her _

Kuß, von Sehn _ _ sucht und Kuß.
ein, zum Fen _ _ ster her _ ein.

Es

Ach! kennst du das Schmach _ ten der

klop _ fen _ den Brust? dies Sin _ nen und Trach _ ten voll Qual und voll

Lust? Be _ flüg _ le die Ei _ le und ret _ te mich dir, ___ bei

nächt _ li _ cher Wei _ le ent _ fliehn wir von hier, bei nächt _ li _ cher

leggiero   cresc.

Wei _ le ent _ fliehn wir von hier.

f   p

Die Se _ gel, sie schwel _ len, die Frucht ist nur
Hei _ mat ent _ flie _ het, so fah _ re sie

p m.v.

Tand: dort, jen _ seit den Wel _ len ist vä _ ter _ lich Land, ist

hin! die Lie _ be, sie zie _ het ge _ wal _ tig den Sinn, ge _

vä _ _ _ ter _ lich Land.

wal _ _ _ tig den Sinn.

Die

Horch! wol _ lü _ stig klin _ gen die Wel _ len im

Meer, sie hüp _ fen und sprin _ gen mut _ wil _ lig ein _ her, und

soll _ ten sie kla _ gen? sie ru _ fen nach dir! __ sie wis _ sen, sie tra _ gen die

Lie _ be von hier, sie wis _ sen, sie tra _ gen die Lie __ be von

hier.

14

lan - - - - - gen.

Die Ster-ne spie - geln sich im Meer, und gol-den glänzt die Flut,

gol den glänzt die Flut.—

gen,   zur längst   er _ sehn _ _ _ _ _ ten _

p cresc.

Hei _ _ _ mat   hin.

In

calmato

lieber, däm _ mernder   Fer _ ne,   dort   ru _ fen hei _ mi _ sche Lie _ der,   aus

dolce

zu der viel - ge - lieb - ten Schwel - - le, end - lich,

p cresc.

end - - - lich mei - - - nem Glück — ent - ge - - - gen,

end - - - lich, end - - - lich mei - nem Glück — ent -

ge - - - - - - - - gen!

f

f

15

Ziemlich langsam

Singstimme

Pianoforte

Treu _ e   Lie _ be

dau _ ert lan _ ge,   ü _ ber _ le _ bet   man _ che,   man _ che

Stund,   und kein Zwei _ fel macht sie ban _ ge,   im _ mer bleibt   ihr Mut ge _

sund, __ immer   bleibt, __ immer bleibt   ihr Mut   ge _ sund.

Dräu - en gleich in dich - ten Schaa - ren, for - dern

gleich zum Wan - kel - mut Sturm und Tod, setzt den Ge -

fah - ren Lieb _____ ent - ge - gen treu - - es _____

Blut.

Und wie Ne - bel stürzt zu - rü - cke, was — den Sinn, — den Sinn — ge - fan - gen hält, und dem hei - tern Früh - lings - bli - cke öff - net sich die wei - te Welt, — öff - net sich, — öff - net sich die wei - te, wei - - - te Welt.

Lebhaft

Er - run - gen, be - zwun - gen von Lieb ist das Glück,_

ver - schwunden die Stun - den, sie flie - hen zu -

rück; und se - li - ge Lust, sie stil - let, er - fül - let die

trun - ke - ne, won - ne - klop - fen - de Brust,_____ sie schei - de von

ad libit.   a Tempo

Lei - de auf im - - - mer, und nim - - - mer, und nim - - - mer, und nim - mer ent - schwinde, und nim - mer ent - schwin - de die lieb - li - che, se - li - ge, himm - li - sche Lust, die himm - li - sche Lust! Sie